© Thorpeness Golf Club 2022
No part of this book may be reproduced
or transmitted in any form or by any other
means without the permission in writing
of Thorpeness Golf Club.

ISBN: 978-1-9162106-3-9

Thorpeness Golf Club: The First 100 Years
was edited by Tim Ewart.
Pictures: Mark Alexander Photography;
Leaderboard Photography

Published in 2022 in Great Britain by
18Players. All rights reserved.
18Players is a subsidiary of Sports
Publications Limited,
2 Arena Park, Leeds, LS17 9BF.
sports-publications.com

About 18Players
18Players is a creative agency specialising
in golf publishing across magazines, books
and digital formats.

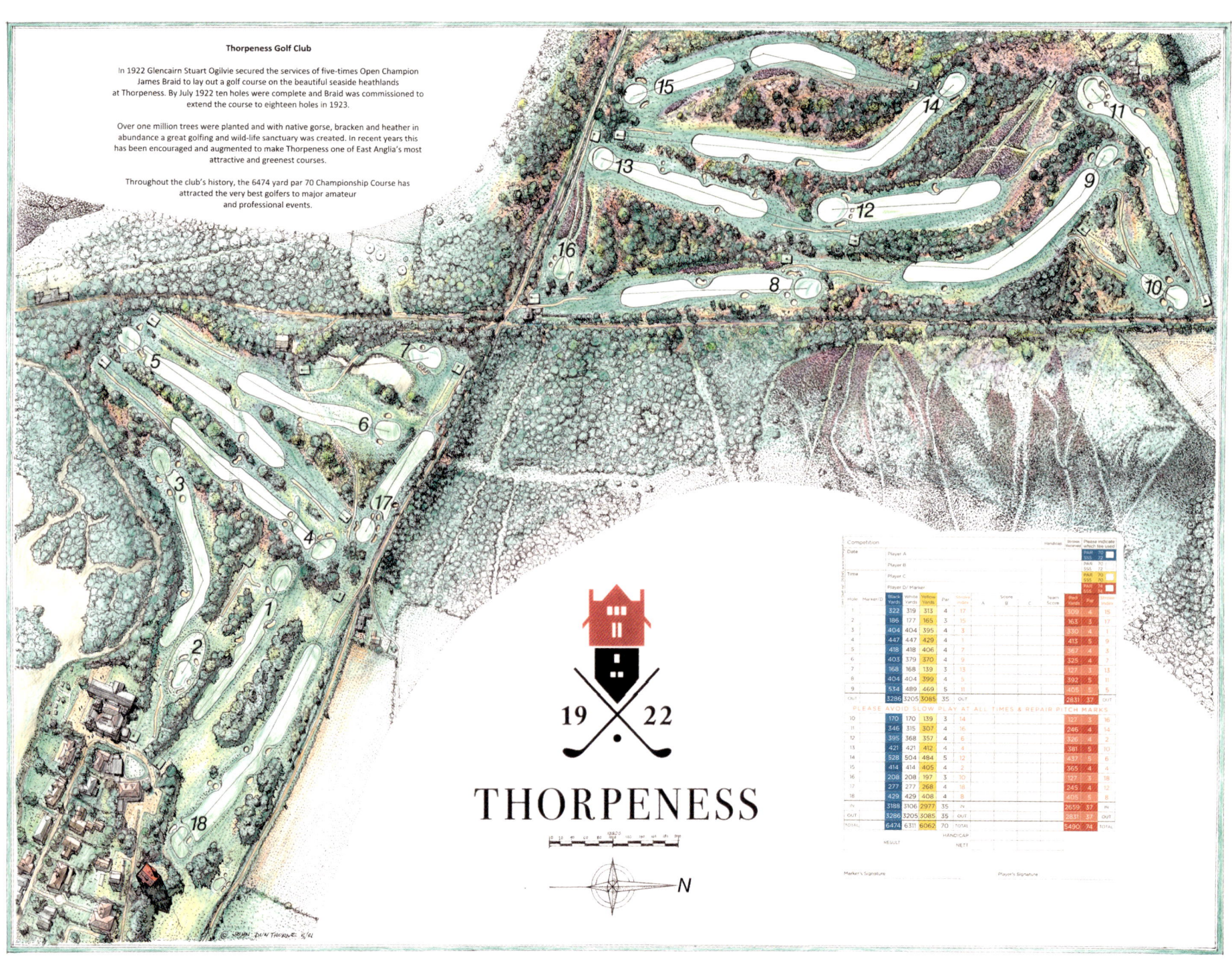

Foreword

The late Peter Alliss, for so long the voice of golf, described Thorpeness Golf Club as "a hidden gem in the Suffolk countryside". After a visit in 1991, he wrote to the then owner, Alec Stenson: "I can't wait to get back and try it again."

It is a sentiment shared by so many who have played this intriguing course and fallen in love with it.

Thorpeness can be a fickle lover. When the sun shines, the breeze is light and the gorse and the bracken are dressed to kill, it is a wonderful place to savour the game. But when the wind blows and the rough bares its teeth, the course can break the bravest of golfing hearts.

The clubhouse has celebrated triumphs and drowned sorrows in equal measure over the years, and its atmosphere has always been a central part of the Thorpeness experience.

As a longstanding member once explained to a guest who wondered if he could have a double gin and tonic: "At this club, dear boy, if you only want a single you have to ask for it."

Thorpeness has welcomed some fascinating characters, visitors as well as members. I wish there was room in what follows to mention them all, but there is not. To those I have left out, my apologies. My thanks to all those who have helped me, not least the late Michael Wood who compiled a history of the club in 2010, and club archivist Tim Garner, who has done so much research.

And I am particularly grateful to Glen Ogilvie, whose great-grandfather made it all possible a century ago. Glen provided fascinating insights into the history of his family, but sadly died just as this book was being completed. **– Tim Ewart, 2022**

🏠 The famous, iconic House in the Clouds has the best view of Thorpeness's 18th green.

THORPENESS

About the author

Tim Ewart was born in Suffolk and learned golf at Woodbridge as a boy. He first played at Thorpeness in 1960 in the Under 12s section of the junior championships, finishing second to one of the club's future owners. After working for many years as a correspondent for ITN he is now retired and living back in his home county.

FIELD OF DREAMS

Contents

FOREWORD 5

CHAPTER 1: 10
IN THE BEGINNING
CARS, RAILWAYS AND
A NEW SEASIDE RESORT

CHAPTER 2: 20
BETWEEN THE WARS
COURSE RECORDS AND
A NEW CLUBHOUSE

CHAPTER 3: 32
WINNING THE PEACE
RECOVERY

CHAPTER 4: 44
THE WINDS OF CHANGE
NEW OWNERSHIP

CHAPTER 5: 54
THE NEW MILLENNIUM
APPROACHING A CENTURY

The well-protected green at the short par-4 17th. Eagles are possible but so too ruinous scores.

Dawn breaks over the 1st green, as another heavenly day on the links at Thorpeness begins.

FIELD OF DREAMS

Chapter 1

IN THE BEGINNING
CARS, RAILWAYS AND A NEW SEASIDE RESORT

Glencairn Stuart Ogilvie, the man they called GSO. The founder of Thorpeness and its golf course. Portrait by J.Cecil Gould.

The man who started it all was not himself a golfer. His family would say he had a clubhouse designed so he could sit on the veranda and gaze out over his beloved Meare, the boating lake that lies at the heart of Thorpeness. His name was Glencairn Stuart Ogilvie, known to friends and family as Stuart, or simply GSO.

The Ogilvie story is part of Suffolk history, and after more than a century the place that GSO built still has the feel of a faintly unreal wonderland. When the sun shines on the Meare, and on the fairways that run beside it, Thorpeness can seem somehow apart from the world outside. And that, of course, is exactly what GSO wanted.

The story really begins with his father, Alexander Milne Ogilvie, a civil engineer who rode the wave of 19th-century industrial expansion with bewildering success. Alexander was a Scotsman who headed south to make his fortune. He did so in partnership with another engineer, Thomas Brassey, and together they built

🏠 Sholto Ogilvie, a decorated soldier in World War I and head of the family business from 1932 until his death in 1960. Portrait by Frank O Salisbury, 1946.

railways across England and around the world, from Mauritius to Russia and Argentina.

Alexander's travels ended in Leiston, just up the road from Thorpeness, where he and his wife Margaret set up home in what became known as Sizewell Hall. It has since been turned into a Christian conference centre, but in the latter half of the 19th century it was at the heart of an estate that grew to cover 6,000 acres along the Suffolk coast.

By the time of the 1861 census, Alexander was no longer officially described as a railway engineer, but a 'gentleman landowner'.

He died in 1886 and was survived by seven of his eight children. His death triggered family discord that rumbled on for more than two decades and became increasingly acrimonious.

It was, inevitably, about money. And there was a lot of money to fight over. The Ogilvie estate, which included land

FIELD OF DREAMS

Soldiers relaxing at Thorpeness Meare during World War I. The Meare remained open throughout the war.

in Scotland as well as Suffolk, was valued at £747,801. No two calculations about what that represents in today's terms are the same, but the Bank of England inflation index puts it very close to £100m. Alexander left it all to his widow, Margaret.

The Ogilvies had always been philanthropists and Margaret continued the tradition. Large sums were bestowed on organisations helping those in need such as sick children, the disadvantaged elderly and shipwrecked sailors. Ogilvie alms houses exist to this day. Her charity did not, however, begin at home. Margaret believed that her children should make their own way, a view that put her at odds with the oldest five.

By the time she died in 1908, much of the family's money had gone, but the land remained. At the reading of her will it was revealed that only the two youngest children were beneficiaries. The Ogilvie estate in Scotland would go to Fergus Monteith, and Glencairn Stuart would have everything in Suffolk. Margaret had disinherited the others and they took legal action.

The challenge to Margaret's will was described in court as 'futile and wasteful' and quickly dismissed. But there followed a second, much more serious case, disputing the original will of her husband. It included a claim that, at the time he made the will, Alexander Milne Ogilvie had not been of sound mind and was under the 'undue influence' of his wife. It was heard in the High Court before a judge and jury, where it was eventually thrown out, confirming Glencairn Stuart Ogilvie as the owner of the family's Suffolk land.

It was a canvas on which he could let his imagination run free. And GSO was certainly blessed with imagination.

If his father had been relentlessly hard-working and little given to socialising, GSO's own interests were altogether more ethereal. He qualified as a barrister but never went into practice, working instead as a playwright. His friends included the novelist JM Barrie, creator of Peter Pan, and the actor Henry Irving.

Margaret Ogilvie died in 1908, dividing the family fortune between her two youngest sons. It caused a bitter family feud that ended in the High Court.

FIELD OF DREAMS

The golf club's first professional John Cassidy with his trusty terrier Prince. Dogs are still allowed on the course but must be 'well behaved.'

GSO's most successful play was a grand production called Hypatia, based on the tragic life of a fifth-century philosopher. It was staged at the Haymarket Theatre in London in 1893 with Julia Nelson, a leading actress of the day, in the title role. A review in the New York Times described her as a 'central point of loveliness' and the production as a 'sumptuous spectacle'.

But GSO had an even more ambitious production in mind, set on a very different kind of stage.

The fishing village of Thorpe lay on the Suffolk coast just south of Sizewell Hall. Once a busy port, there was not much left by the turn of the 20th century. Several of its houses had been swallowed up by the encroaching North Sea, and it was surrounded by marshland. Its residents could see little future. But not GSO. He saw Thorpeness.

He sketched out his plans, bought the village and set to work creating his perfect seaside resort. There would be nothing ostentatious – no piers nor promenades nor grand hotels – but rather houses built in Tudor style to reflect a bygone age. It would be particularly attractive to wealthy visitors from London.

GSO envisioned the centrepiece of this idyllic holiday world when he gazed out over the mist-shrouded marshes one morning in 1910. There would be a mere, a boating lake where children could let their imaginations run riot. Narrow channels would divide areas of water called the Caribbean Sea, the Spanish Main and the Blue Lagoon. There would be Crusoe's Island, Wendy's House and Peter Pan's Property. And the mere would be The Meare, using the original Elizabethan spelling.

It was dug out by hand, all 64 acres, much of the work done by local fishermen on what were called 'nor'easters', days when the prevailing wind prevented their boats taking to the sea.

Three years later, GSO declared that work should start on another compelling attraction in the new Thorpeness: a golf course. It may have been a sport that

James Braid marking out the original first green in 1922. Looking on is A.J. "Grandpa" Barclay who in 1926 presented the cup that bears his name.

held no interest to him personally, but he recognised its growing popularity and knew the appeal it would add to his holiday world.

Golf had been played in Scotland since the 15th century, but it was a slow starter south of the border. When a course was opened in 1880 on the Suffolk coast at Felixstowe, it was only the fifth in England. Within 20 years there were more than 500.

It was all down to technology. As the nineteenth century drew to a close, people were on the move as never before. Those who could afford it, drove. The first British car had been built in 1892, and by 1910 there were 100,000 on the road. The rail network, in which GSO's father had played such a pivotal role, had expanded rapidly. It included a station called Thorpeness Halt, just behind what is now the 8th tee.

Golf equipment was suddenly more accessible too. The hand-crafted clubs of the early days were being replaced by mass production. The golf ball evolved from the expensive featherie, made from hand-stitched leather stuffed with goose feathers, to a guttie that was made from tree sap and, finally, at the turn of the century, to a ball with a rubber core.

Thorpeness golf course looked very different back then, an expanse of barren heathland with hardly a tree to be seen. But GSO was a visionary and he ordered work to begin. His chosen designer was Harry Colt, a course architect whose portfolio included Wentworth, Sunningdale New and Muirfield. Here was the man to turn the Ogilvie vision into reality.

The year was 1913, and within a few months work had stopped. The world was at war.

For the Ogilvies, like hundreds of thousands of other families, it was a war that brought personal tragedy. GSO's two sons joined the army. The youngest, Sholto, was captured and reported missing presumed dead after an escape attempt from a German prison camp.
A month later came the news that he had been re-captured. Sholto survived, but his brother did not.

FIELD OF DREAMS

Lieutenant Alexander Ogilvie was an artillery officer caught in a mustard gas attack near Arras. A gun became stuck in muddy ground and in the confusion he removed his gas mask so his orders could be more clearly heard. Alexander was poisoned and died in hospital on October 30, 1918. The war ended 11 days later.

The resort of Thorpeness had attracted enough wartime visitors to keep the business afloat.

And for all his personal sadness, GSO pressed ahead. Work on the golf course had been suspended, but plans were resurrected, and another renowned architect hired.

Like Colt, James Braid is among the most celebrated of Britain's golf course designers. He was an outstanding player, winning five Open Championships, two of them by a six-shot lead.

He worked on some 400 courses, including Felixstowe, Woodbridge and Ipswich.

Braid produced an initial layout of 10 holes at Thorpeness and submitted a bill for £12.

The work was supervised by the club's first professional, John Cassidy. Cassidy was a Liverpudlian and one of three brothers, all professional golfers.

He learned his trade at Hoylake under the tutorship of Jack Morris, a member of the renowned St Andrews golfing family. Cassidy was hired from Aldeburgh Golf Club, where he had been the professional since 1908.

Work on Thorpeness golf course was carried out by hand, as it had been on the Meare 10 years before. Cassidy supervised a team of 90 and they must have set about the job with extraordinary determination. It began in the spring of 1922 and by July James Braid's 10 holes were completed. GSO ordered the planting of thousands of trees in and around Thorpeness, and the heathland was slowly transformed into the beautiful setting it is today.

Ten holes were not, of course, enough for GSO. He wanted the best. Within a year eight more had been added, finishing at The Pavilion, the original clubhouse.

🏠 A place where the sun always shines. Early posters for the new Thorpeness resort.

It was built at the end of what is now the practice ground and is there to this day as a private home.

Overlooking it all was the House in the Clouds, originally a water tower with a cleverly disguised 50,000 gallon tank perched above living accommodation on the four floors below.

The water tank has now gone, but the House in the Clouds looks as it always did. The fifth-floor games room with stunning views makes it a much sought-after holiday rental.

Thorpeness was complete, a little fishing village transformed into one of the country's most beguiling holiday resorts. An advertisement in The Times in 1923 described it as 'the garden village 'twixt lake and sea'. Its attractions were listed as safe bathing, golden sands, a large ballroom, tennis courts and an 18-hole golf course.

There were difficult times ahead, but Glencairn Stuart Ogilvie had finally created his very own field of dreams. 🏠

The opening tee shot. Golfers enjoy a warm Thorpeness welcome in the starter's hut before tackling the par-4 1st.

FIELD OF DREAMS

Chapter 2

BETWEEN THE WARS
COURSE RECORDS AND A NEW CLUBHOUSE

Turning dreams into reality can be expensive. It is Thorpeness Golf Club's good fortune that GSO was not a man to let financial obstacles stand in his way.

If the Roaring Twenties were a time to shake off the miseries of war, they were also the precursor to a decade of economic recession. Thorpeness was still a magnet for well-heeled visitors, but it was a seasonal trade and there was evidence that people were being more careful with their money. There were those in GSO's management team who advised caution. Spending should be reined in, and projects shelved. There was even a suggestion that the golf course itself should be put up for sale.

It fell on deaf ears. GSO believed that only by offering the best facilities could Thorpeness maintain its appeal. Houses should be of the highest standard, with the Meare and the surrounding open spaces perfectly maintained.

The new Golf Club House, 1930

Most radically, the golf club would be taken to a different level with a smart new clubhouse. The original pavilion was a modest building and GSO wanted something altogether more eye-catching. It came in the form of a Spanish-style country house, dominated by four turrets, and standing at the top of a sweeping driveway. It cost £5,200 and GSO was sure the expense would be justified by the attention it would attract. He was right.

The clubhouse was opened in grand style on April 30, 1930, with a six-course lunch for 52 guests.

One sentence in GSO's welcoming speech captured the ethos that had driven his life: "The sole ambition of every artist is to leave this sordid world of ours the more beautiful for his coming."

Sadly, GSO did not have much longer to enjoy his drinks on the clubhouse terrace. He died two years later and a new generation of Ogilvies took control. The business was to be run by GSO's son

The clubhouse shortly after it was completed in 1930 at a cost of £5,200. Visitors could buy weekly membership for 20 shillings, the equivalent of one pound.

FIELD OF DREAMS

The lunch to celebrate the clubhouse opening. The man standing in the centre of the top table is Sir Herbert Hambling, presenter of the Hambling Vase. To his left is the founder, Glencairn Stuart Ogilvie.

Sholto, but his heir was his grandson, Alexander Stuart, whose father had died in the war.

Whatever the finances of its owners, Thorpeness had secured its place on the golfing map. There were glowing reviews in newspapers and magazines from as far afield as India and Canada, and British journalists became regular visitors.

Out on the course, what we think of as modern golf was in its infancy. The new stars, men like Bobby Jones and Walter Hagen, had brought a swashbuckling excitement to the game. At Thorpeness, a schoolmaster called Walter Winstanley captured the spirit of the age. Winstanley, known to everyone as Winston, had a double first from Cambridge and taught English and history at Framlingham College. He set great store by learning and would dismiss those less intelligent as 'vulgarians'. He was also an outstanding sportsman, a cricket coach and a scratch golfer. There are still stories told of how

Walter Winstanley with pipe, collar and tie – and the classic follow-through. Perhaps the finest golfer in the club's history.

he once drove the 6th hole at Thorpeness, now a 379-yard par 4 and probably of similar length in those early days.

The original course record was set by John Cassidy, the club's first professional, with a 73. It was beaten in 1927 by the Great Yarmouth pro Clifford Holland, with a score of 71. Walter Winstanley equalled that mark in 1935, but two years later the Framlingham News reported a round by Winstanley that makes extraordinary reading to this day.

His card contained just one five, on the 12th hole. A front nine of 32 was followed by 33, giving a 10-under-par total of 65. It appears not to have been recognised as a course record, almost certainly because it was not in a competition.

Walter Winstanley used hickory-shafted clubs and played in collar and tie, a pipe clenched firmly between his teeth. But his style mirrored the teaching of the day. When golf balls were stuffed with feathers and hit with long-nosed woods, they were

FIELD OF DREAMS

🏠 The original 1st green, now the 3rd, on the edge of the Meare.

struck with a flat, sweeping swing to keep them low and rolling. By the 1920s, golfers were more upright, more aggressive and more capable of hitting a draw.

What was crucially lacking in their clubs was forgiveness. Shots struck off-centre, from the toe or heel, were harshly punished.

Those who study the science of golf estimate that a mishit from a persimmon driver would have travelled about 40 yards less than the same bad shot from a modern club, and most certainly would not have held its line.

This need for precision, the importance of hitting the ball 'out of the screws' on that tiny sweet spot on the clubface, widened the gap between the few low-handicappers and the rest.

The first monthly medal recorded in the Thorpeness competition book was won by D Brown, handicap two.

Of the other 11 entries, seven were no-returns.

Thorpeness Golf Club: The First 100 Years **1922-2022**

🏠 The Silver Frigate takes pride of place among the Thorpeness trophies. It was presented in 1931.

Walter Winstanley was arguably the finest golfer in the club's history.

He kept a scratch handicap for many years, and his name appears on the Thorpeness trophy boards over a period spanning four decades, from 1931 to 1961.

Much later, in more troubled times, those splendid silver trophies were to be given a scrap value of £3,000.

Whatever they may have fetched in a sale room, the history they hold and the stories they tell far outweigh any monetary value.

The first, presented in 1923, was the Ogilvie Shield, named after the club's founder.

Many of the trophies that followed bear the names of the personalities he attracted to Thorpeness.

Andrew Barclay, a maths teacher affectionately known as Grandpa, had a holiday home across the road from the Meare.

He was GSO's vice-president and club secretary. The Barclay Cup dates back to 1926.

Percy Neale presented the cup that bears his name in 1929. Born in Camden Town, in London, he had taken his summer holidays in Thorpeness since the First World War.

George Kite was in the shipping business and also came from London. He rented a holiday home overlooking the beach at Thorpeness. The Kite Cup was first contested in 1930, as was the Hambling Vase.

Sir Herbert Hambling had presided over the opening of the new clubhouse and succeeded GSO as club president.

Stanley Mallinson made his money from timber, lived in Bury St Edmunds and spent his summers in a house called Rudder Grange, a stone's throw from the Thorpeness clubhouse. Stanley liked to play golf in style, and his chauffeur would pack the boot of the car with food and drink and meet him behind the old 9th green, now the 7th.

Golfers from around the country have competed for the Mallinson Silver Frigate since 1931, and there have been some

FIELD OF DREAMS

Golf fashion between the wars: flat caps and plus-fours. This was the old 1st tee in 1930.

memorable rounds. Walter Winstanley's official course record was broken in 1937 by AJ Garland, a +1 golfer from Royal Wimbledon. His 69 included nine birdies.

The earliest written records of the club date back to April 1924, and a meeting of the ladies' committee. The minutes were taken in immaculate copperplate handwriting and recorded discussions about planned competitions. It seems the first lady members confined deliberations to their own golfing matters. Other issues were left to the men.

The first surviving minutes of the main club committee are from August 1936, when it was decided to create new bunkers on the 11th and 12th fairways. Many changes had been made since John Cassidy and his men set to work all those years earlier, and in 1937 it was declared that the course had 'improved out of all knowledge'.

There were challenges, nevertheless. Rabbits were a constant problem, despite the attention of a warrener, or gamekeeper. There was talk of fencing in the whole course, and in 1938 local rules were amended to permit a free drop from a rabbit scrape.

There was also the vexing matter of dogs on the course. Alarm was voiced that one member, Mr Barlow, had written to The Field magazine saying he had trained his dog to retrieve golf balls, and it had found 171 on three holes. It was felt this might discourage people from coming to the course.

Membership fees had been set at three guineas a year for men (the equivalent of £3.15) and two guineas for ladies.

In 1938 it was agreed there should be a new category, the artisan.

Members of the Alexander Ogilvie Workmen's Club would be 'granted the privilege' of playing on the course for an annual fee of 10 shillings and sixpence (52p). They were limited to certain starting times and could not enter the clubhouse or its surroundings.

For the full members, two areas of awkwardness were dealt with. Tipping in the clubhouse was deemed 'irregular' and banned for all but visitors and temporary members.

It was further agreed that anyone getting a hole in one, and there have been many at Thorpeness, should 'not be penalised by having to stand drinks all round'. They would instead receive a silver matchbox, suitably inscribed.

On July 1, 1939, two months before the outbreak of war, the impending international crisis finally cast a shadow over the affairs of the club. An army officer, Colonel Henderson, had agreed to take on the role of secretary but felt that, 'owing to the political situation', he would not be free until the following December.

War was declared on September 3, 1939, and the committee decided to close the seven holes on the far side of the road that divides the course. Serving officers were given honorary membership for the duration of hostilities.

The following month, with staff numbers already reduced, the steward was dismissed for 'grave irregularities' after £30 went missing from the Christmas fund. The club professional was also released.

Two years earlier, JD Freeman had been the Suffolk Open champion but, as savings were made, he was asked to work as a groundsman. He was clearly unhappy and deemed guilty of not 'punching his weight'.

The committee met for the last time just before Christmas in 1939. There was some optimism amid the gloom.

The 11 holes that remained open had been well maintained, and the minutes contained a final note: "The feeling of the committee was that at any rate until about March it should be possible to keep the whole course in a playable condition."

It was an accurate prediction. On March 25, 1940, 20 members turned out for the monthly medal.

In France, the British Expeditionary Force was being driven back towards the beaches of Dunkirk and the war was taking an ominous turn. There was to be no more golf for a while.

The par-3 7th is perhaps Thorpeness's prettiest and most eye-catching hole.

Thorpeness Golf Club: The First 100 Years **1922-2022**

An aerial view

OF THORPENESS

1. Lakeside Suite and hotel rooms
2. Thorpeness GC clubhouse
3. Ogilvie Restaurant and superior rooms
4. Pro shop and putting green
5. Braid Lodge hotel rooms
6. Lakeside Avenue
7. The Boathouse and Meare
8. The North Sea
9. The Country Club, Tennis Court and The Infantry
10. Practice area, formerly 17th & 18th holes
11. Ogilvie Hall*
12. Margaret Ogilvie Almshouses
13. The Windmill
14. House in the Clouds
15. The Whinlands

* Originally built in 1925 as a theatre for GSO's plays. Became Thorpeness Sports and Social Club which was later transferred to the pavilion.

FIELD OF DREAMS

Chapter 3

WINNING THE PEACE
RECOVERY

Stuart Ogilvie rowing for Oxford in 1935. Known as 'Captain Stuart,' he was the golf club proprietor from 1960 until his death 12 years later.

There are still reminders of war along the Suffolk coast: gun emplacements, concrete pillboxes, tank barriers and even buildings used for top-secret research. But they are a tiny remnant of the defences put up in 1940, when the threat of German invasion was alarmingly real.

The stretch of beach between Aldeburgh and Walberswick, with Thorpeness at its centre, was sewn with 7,500 mines. Sharpened metal 'dragon's teeth' were set along the tideline with barbed wire stretched out behind. Trenches were dug and fields flooded. The wetlands of Minsmere, now a nature reserve, were created in this frantic drive to obstruct the enemy.

Even the railway line that brought so many visitors to Thorpeness and Aldeburgh was part of the defence plan.

An armoured train with a contingent of Polish soldiers was stationed at Saxmundham, ready to head for the coast to reinforce the hundreds of troops already in position.

The Thorpeness Artisans Hambro Cup team in the early 1950s. Left to right: Harold Culff, Jack Middleditch, Ernie Harle, Teddy Block, Herbert Block, Joe Shipp, Jack Staff, Jack Cooper.

A report that formed part of a Mass Observation Survey at the time noted that the economic basis of the area had been wiped out and added that civilians 'wonder whether it will ever be possible to make the beaches nice again'.

The golf club did not escape. The clubhouse was requisitioned by the military and the fairways scarred by anti-tank ditches. It was feared the course would be an ideal landing ground for gliders bringing in German infantry. Fortunately, the greens were spared damage.

Members of the Ogilvie family were again in uniform, and again the family suffered painful loss. Sholto Ogilvie's son, Glencairn, was a Flight Lieutenant in Bomber Command. On the night of December 18, 1940, his Wellington crashed on take-off from Newmarket and exploded in flames. He was one of four flight crew who lost their lives. Two were rescued.

The heir to the Thorpeness business, Alexander Stuart Ogilvie, had gone to South Africa before the war to gain working experience. When hostilities broke out, he joined the Transvaal Horse Artillery. Captain Stuart, as he would be known from then on, fought the German Afrika Korps in the Western Desert and was captured at Tobruk in 1942. He was released when the war ended and returned home to the calmer territory of the golf course he had inherited from his grandfather.

FIELD OF DREAMS

Dennis Levermore in his army uniform. Dennis became the club professional in 1946, a job he held until his death in 1964.

Among the Thorpeness members to return from war was Balfour Hutchison. He had fought with the 7th Hussars in the First World War and had a holiday home in Aldeburgh. He was a four-handicap golfer whose name appears three times on the trophy boards. Balfour Hutchison began the Second World War as a colonel, served in in the Middle East, North Africa and India, and was promoted to Lieutenant General. Two of his sons, Andrew and Julian, were killed in action. They were both 20 when they died.

The club committee re-assembled on August 18, 1945, three months after the end of the war in Europe. The course was still closed, but at least it was back to business.

The minutes of the last meeting, some six years earlier, were duly read and passed. A cordial welcome was extended to Captain Stuart Ogilvie, who announced that, despite the considerable damage caused by the military, pre-war plans to improve the course would go ahead. It was agreed that a deep anti-tank ditch near the railway station should be covered in rabbit wire and deemed an 'advantageous hazard', allowing a free drop.

In April 1946, 10 members took part in the first post-war competition, the Easter Monday medal. The following year the men challenged the ladies and were soundly beaten. The first match that day pitted a husband against his wife and, rather embarrassingly, was over on the 13th green. Mrs Robinson defeated her husband 6 and 5.

Walter Winstanley, who had been such a dominant force at the club in the pre-war years, was still a scratch golfer but was held to a tie. His opponent was Gertie Scott, one of the great characters in the ladies' section.

Gertie was part of the Mallinson family, presenters of the Silver Frigate. She had served in the Women's Royal Air Force in the war and married a Group Captain, George Scott. They returned to run the Dolphin Hotel in Thorpeness and Group Captain Scott became a well-liked club secretary. His initials were GFL, which earned him the nickname 'Gone For

Lunch'. Silver ashtrays given to his wife in the 1940s were donated to the club, and the Gertie Scott Ashtrays are still played for in an annual mixed foursomes competition.

The committee may have had the events of that 1947 match in mind when a decision was taken to address the rights of women golfers. Section 10 of the book of rules read: Ladies playing together or with gentlemen should allow gentlemen to pass when it is manifest that the latter are being kept back. Now the club captain declared that "men could not keep up the pretence of being better golfers than the ladies". Section 10 was deleted.

Life at the club gradually returned to normal. The clubhouse, left in poor condition after military occupation, was restored to its former glory. Dennis Levermore was appointed the new professional and Thorpeness was again attracting the attention it had enjoyed in the 1930s.

When a writer from Golf Illustrated stepped off the train at Thorpeness Halt station one July morning in 1949, Captain Stuart Ogilvie was waiting to greet him, black Labrador at his side. Lessons in public relations passed down from his grandfather had been well learned. The magazine duly described Thorpeness as 'an earthly paradise' and its golf course 'as pretty and sporting as you can find anywhere in the country'.

Attracting new members remained a challenge. Traffic on the course was light in the summer – and in the winter it was often deserted. As the club re-opened after the war there were barely 260 members, 17 of them originals from 1922. But as new golfers arrived, others resigned or passed away. A decade later there were still only 273 members, 49 of them ladies. The annual subscription was nine guineas for men, and a guinea less for women, but there was a significant reduction for one group the club was keen to attract: American service personnel.

The World Wars had been replaced by the Cold War, and Suffolk was on the front line. The 81st Fighter Wing of the United States Air Force had bases nearby at RAF Bentwaters and RAF Woodbridge. Anyone who played on local courses in those days will have vivid memories of the American golfers. They were affable and competitive, and liked side bets that were generally too rich for their British hosts.

Sholto Ogilvie, in his role as club president, had welcomed the Americans as 'good neighbours and very good friends of ours', but, in 1957. two incidents threatened to undermine the special relationship.

The first was on the course. It happened on the 16th hole when two members frustrated by a slow American group on the fairway ahead shouted fore and drove off. Committee minutes record that one of the Americans marched up to a ball that had landed nearby and hit it straight back to the tee. Another threatened the offending member with 'the biggest hiding he had ever had in his life'.

A request for a Bentwaters golf day later in the year also ended badly. The sticking

FIELD OF DREAMS

The view of the clubhouse from the third hole, before the annexe was built for hotel guests.

point was the proposal for a Texas-style barbecue and morning cocktails to get golfers in the right mood. The club would go no further than sandwiches and drinks in the clubhouse after the match. The ensuing argument involved what the club secretary described as 'filthy language'. An American officer was ordered to leave.

Peace was quickly restored. Two months later five more US Air Force officers were admitted as members, with a suggestion from their colonel that they should be trained in 'club and course etiquette'.

There had by then been change at the top. Sholto Ogilvie stepped down through ill health and died in 1960. He had run the Ogilvie business for 28 years and overseen the revival of the golf club after the war. He was replaced by his nephew Captain Stuart, a popular figure with a love of sport and the social life that went with it.

Stuart enjoyed cricket and tennis and had been an accomplished oarsman, first reserve for the Oxford blues at two boat races. He had tried his hand at golf in South Africa before the war but lost interest in it, until his son Glen found a canvas bag of hickory clubs hanging in the gun room at their home. He insisted his father should take him out for a game.

It started on the 8th hole and finished in the bar of the Dolphin Hotel. Stuart did not want anyone to know he played until he was good enough to avoid embarrassment. It did not take long. Captain Stuart was soon a regular and

Lady golfers on the 6th green shortly after the war. In the background, the 7th and old railway station.

enthusiastic golfer, adding his name to the trophy boards in the clubhouse.

A plan for significant changes to the course had first been suggested and approved in the mid-1950s. It involved removing the 17th and 18th holes. The late Michael Wood, who wrote a history of the club in 2010, described the 17th as a particularly unpopular 'long slog' running up to a green beneath the House in the Clouds.

The club gained a practice ground when the two holes were removed.

The holes that replaced them were designed by the golf course architect Ken Cotton and became the 14th and 15th, a par five and a par four. Both are outstanding holes by any standard. The par three 7th was also improved, with a pond dug between tea and green. It is regarded as one of the best short holes in East Anglia. The changes created a course that stood at 6,241 yards from the back tees and had a par of 69.

It is a measure of the challenge it presented that no one could better a score of 67. That record was set at a 36-hole invitational competition to mark the opening of the new course in May, 1965. Keith MacDonald was the professional at Hankley Common in Surrey and had been the early leader in the 1961 Open Championship at Troon. He scored 67 on both his rounds at Thorpeness.

Three months later, on Captain's Day, the record was equalled by an invited guest who was not entitled to win a prize. Bob Coombes, from Walton Heath, had

FIELD OF DREAMS

Thorpe Halt station, a popular destination when the club was opened, but closed to passengers in 1966.

a handicap of four. He started his round with a five, the first of four bogeys, but birdied six other holes. The course record was not equalled again until the 1980s.

Regular visitors included one of Britain's great wartime heroes, Douglas Bader, who had friends in Thorpeness. Bader lost both legs in an air crash in 1931 but went on to become an ace fighter pilot. His Spitfire was shot down in 1941 and he ended the war as a prisoner at Colditz Castle. He did now allow disability to inhibit his golf and was a fiercely competitive four-handicapper. During one visit to Suffolk he gave a speech to pupils at the old Leiston Modern School and they presented him with a putter cast from brass taps. It is not known if it was ever used.

Bunker rakes made in the school workshop most certainly were used, however. They were the idea of Colin Taylor, a teacher at the school and a keen golfer. He took 74 rakes to the golf club, one for each bunker. It was the first time that rakes had been left out, and it brought an end to the old method of levelling sand with a club, or the spikes of a golf shoe.

It was not Colin Taylor's only innovation. As a new member in 1964 he had waited in vain outside the clubhouse looking for a game, only to be told by the secretary: "It's all diary golf here."

The solution was the first Thorpeness roll-up, started by Taylor and one of the American members.

Fourballs were restricted to the 8th tee, and it was here that the roll-up gathered at 8.30 in the morning on Saturdays and Sundays. Partners were drawn on numbered wooden discs cut from an old chair leg. On a good day, the turnout might reach 24. At the end of the round, they often headed straight from the 7th green to the Parrot pub nearby.

Trevor Youngs joined on his 21st birthday in 1957 and was one of a growing number of members who were not second-home holidaymakers, but lived and worked in Suffolk. Trevor was only admitted to the club after an interview with the five-man membership committee. He played in plus-twos, a streamlined version of the plus-four trousers which were still much in evidence. Gentlemen were required to wear jacket and tie in the clubhouse, and the steward would eject anyone who did not conform to the dress code.

But despite such formality, those who played their golf at Thorpeness at the time recalled a warm and friendly club, where the drink would flow freely and there was a great sense of fun.

The branch railway line that ran through Thorpeness to Aldeburgh stopped taking passengers in 1966. That summer, the club secretary, Group Captain Scott, hired a diesel train with three coaches to provide a buffet lunch of beer and sandwiches at the old station. According to the Daily Mirror, British Rail charged the golf club a total of £30 and still made a profit.

Another train was hired the following year. This time it ran back and forth between Thorpeness and Aldeburgh blowing its whistle as it passed the course. The occasion was the captain's day organised by one of the club's many memorable characters, Owen Ruane. He had joined in 1930 and spent his summers in Thorpeness. He liked the place so much that he named a racehorse after it. Owen died in 1971 but is remembered with the annual foursomes trophy that bears his name.

Other special moments are recorded for posterity in a book called 'It Happened'. There is the day Betty Robson searched for her ball around the 10th green and eventually found it in her hand. She had forgotten to hit a drive. There are stories about the golfer who did drive off, only for the ball to lodge under his left foot, and about the exploits of Richard Long, then the county captain.

His opening drive at an invitation day event cannoned back off the ladies' tee box, over the starter's hut and under a Jaguar at the far end of the car park. The keys were in the car and it was moved. Richard played an 8-iron back over the hut, a 3-wood to the green and two-putted for his five.

Tim Plewman won both the Ogilvie Shield and the Hambling Vase. He was not a man to give in easily. In the 1955 Silver Frigate he lost three successive drives from the 11th tee. Finally, with his fourth attempt, he took seven off the tee, birdied the hole with that ball and finished with a nine.

And if there were ever a lesson about the need to stay straight at Thorpeness, it was learned by Martin Smith in the 1964 Frigate. Martin had a handicap of 18 and struggled round in 100 in the morning, followed by a 'no return' in the afternoon. He lost 14 balls in the process, but still beat his playing partner in their private match.

Golfers love to reminisce about the good old days: warm summer afternoons on the course followed by long evenings at the 19th hole.

The past is often seen through rose-tinted lenses and the 60s were undoubtedly a special time at Thorpeness, a club very much at ease with itself. But as a new decade began, tragedy on the course was to lead to more troubled times.

🏌 Thorpeness's 16th hole is a particularly testing par 3, albeit mercifully does play downhill.

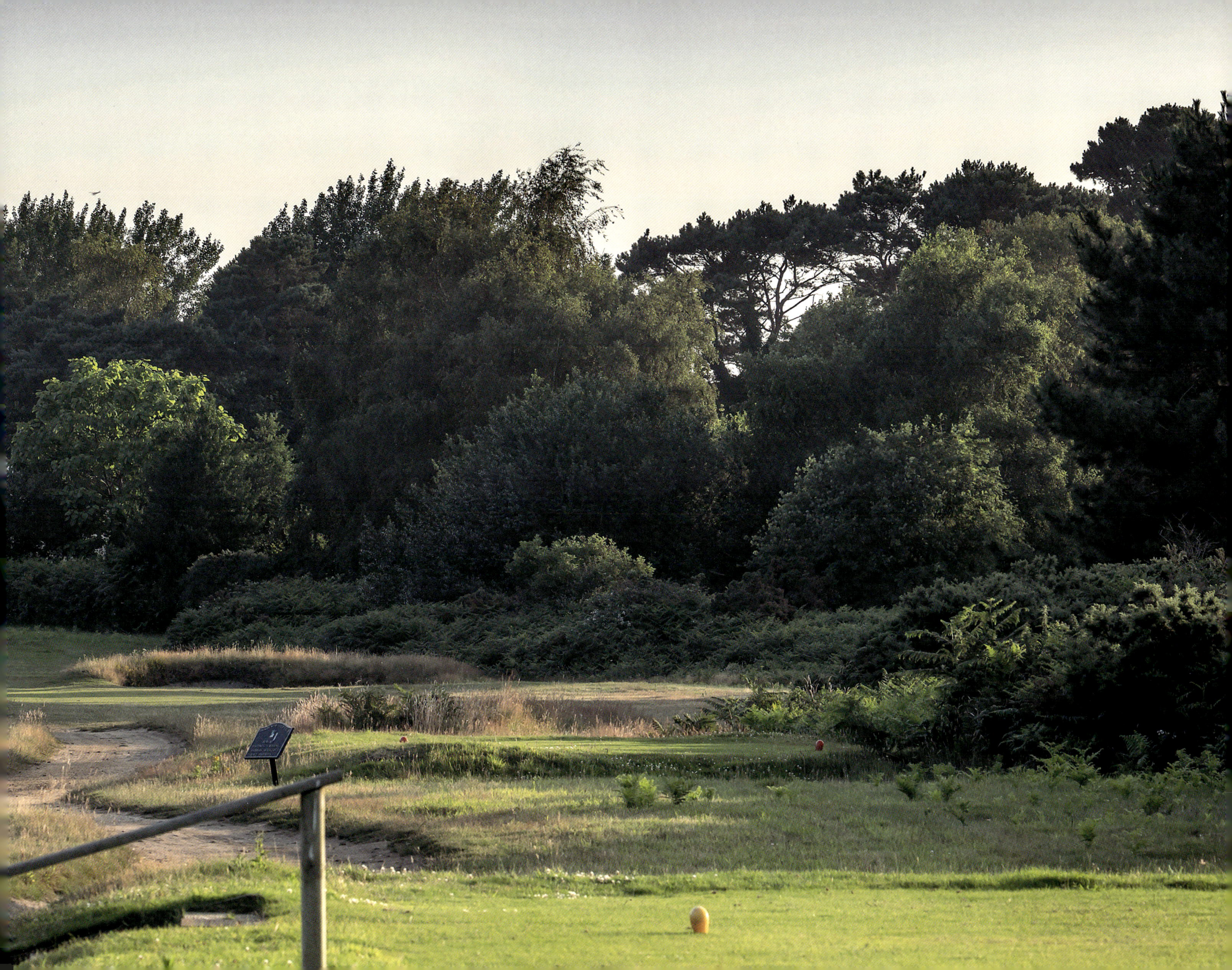

FIELD OF DREAMS

Thorpeness cup winners

1992 Cranworth Trophy team. Back row: Margaret Bolton, Pauline Mayhew, Susan Cooney, Hilary Plant, Marion Stannard. Front row: Pauline Whitrow, Joan Curle (lady captain) Tangy Herron.

2003 Tolley Cobbold Cup team: John Last, James Tilbrook, Jack Thorp, David Hurr, Stuart Tilbrook, James Brinded, Richard Baker, Adrian Whatling, John Cross (club captain), George Skevington, Merv Lambert (team captain), John Curtis.

2006 Parks Trophy team. Richard Newton, Stuart Robson, Merv Lambert, Mick Crabtree, Brian Lindores, Ray Foreman, Mick Cook, Robin Baker, Mick Ellis, David Lloyd.

2012 Tolley Cobbold Cup team: Damon Bloomfield, Mick Crabtree, Stuart Robson (team captain) Chris Scott (club captain), Robin Baker, Matt Crane, Sean Clemments, Mick Ellis, Steve Mew, Jon Last, Mick Squirrell, Mick Cook, Jack Levermore, Lee Newson, Andrew Whiting, Sam Newson.

Thorpeness Golf Club: The First 100 Years **1922-2022**

1993 Cranworth Trophy team. Back row: Pauline Mayhew, Susan Cooney, Elisabeth Lindores. Front row: Pauline Whitrow, Joan Salter (lady captain), Tangy Herron.

2002 Parks Trophy team: Robin Baker, Richard Newton, Frank Dutton, Merv Lambert, Brian Lindores, John Curtis, Erik Duckworth, George Skevington, Chris Scott, Robin Ellisfaude.

2002 Parks Trophy. Robin Baker receives the trophy from Maurice Parks, president of the Suffolk Golf Union.

2018 Parks Trophy team. Tony Mardon, Roger Brown (senior captain), Jon Last, David Brown, Richard Newton (club president), Ray Foreman (team captain), Robert Ayrton, Colin Firmin (SGU president), Peter Cooney, Mick Ford, Mick Cook.

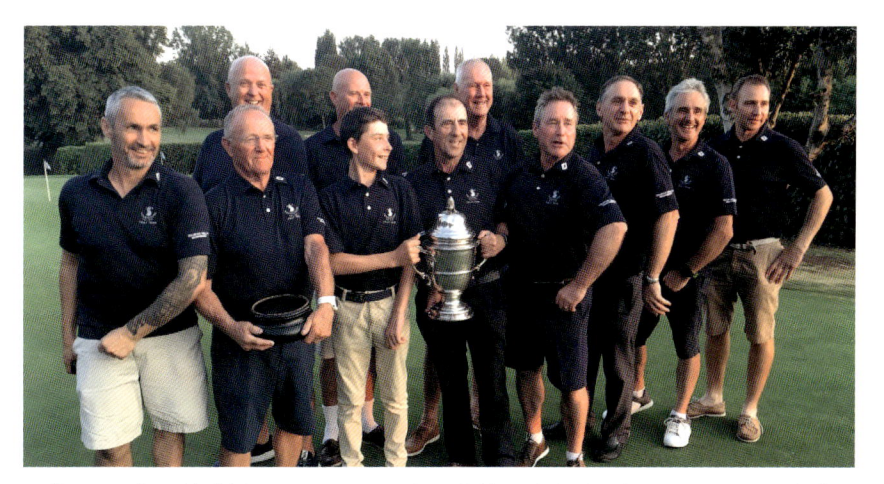

2019 Tolly Cobbold Cup team. Damon Bloomfield, Mick Cook, Chris May, Harry Brinded, Peter Cooney, Bob Booker, Richard Newton, Roger Brown, Graham Denny, Sean Clements, James Tilbrook (Tolly team captain).

45

Chapter 4

THE WINDS OF CHANGE
NEW OWNERSHIP

Captain Stuart Ogilvie died on September 5, 1972. He was 57 years old. It was a perfect late summer day, and Stuart was paired with his son, Glen, in a foursomes against club member Bob Wallace and the former cabinet minister Bill Deedes, later to become editor of the Daily Telegraph. Glen drove first, playing a 3-wood for safety, but hooked the ball into a bed of lupins that used to grow beside the 1st fairway.

Glen set off to look for his ball, leaving his father to play a provisional. It was the last shot Stuart was to hit. As walked down the fairway he collapsed, and although he sat up for a moment and said 'I'm alright' he had suffered a fatal heart attack.

Members mourned his loss. He was an endearing character and good company both on the course and in the bar, where he liked to sit with a pint of 'built up', a mixture of bitter and pale ale.

The ladies' captain, Audrey Deth, perhaps best summed up his popularity,

Glen Ogilvie, who took over the club in 1972 but was eventually forced to sell. This picture was taken in 2012. Glen died in July, 2021.

telling her committee: "What a splendid man he was and how he will be missed by everyone."

For Glen Ogilvie, his father's premature death was more than a personal tragedy. It was the beginning of a decade of mounting financial difficulties that, at the age of 23, he had been ill-prepared to handle. It soon became apparent that he faced crippling estate duty, a tax obligation that could only be met by the sale of property. Nearly all of Thorpeness was put on the market.

For a time, it seemed that the Ogilvie dynasty would continue. Glen became club president and as his golf improved he enjoyed success in several competitions. But storms clouds were gathering.

By the spring of 1977, concerns about the future of the club prompted him to outline to the committee his position over death duties. A notice was posted to assure members that the club would continue to function, but the following month things began to look rather different.

Seventeen legendary ladies. A picture from 1986 of former lady captains. L-R, standing: Jean Cooksey, Flo Unstead, Nell Richworth, Gertie Scott, Eilen Aylott, Jean Barent, Tangy Herron, Lorraine Greenoak, Joan Dibble, Frances Dodman, Anne Holland, Pat Sneath. Seated: Phyllis Grounwater, Betty Robson, Gwen Dennison, Pat Jacombhood, Grace Agate.

FIELD OF DREAMS

The original Thorpeness 'four ballers.' L-R, standing: Roly Watson, Ralph Werner. Seated: Derek Hammond-Giles, Roy Fishwick, Bob Unstead, Richard Thompson.

George Phillips was the liquidator appointed by the Ogilvies to resolve the crisis faced by the family business. On May 6, 1977, he told the committee the club was for sale. The initial asking price was £125,000, with some strings attached. The freehold would be retained by Glen and two other trustees, and the use of the land restricted to golf. A sub-committee formed to consider the purchase concluded the liquidator's valuation was too high.

There has been considerable debate over the years as to whether the members of Thorpeness Golf Club let a golden opportunity slip through their fingers. The late Bob Curle, who ran an electrical business in Snape, was devoted to the club and a prime mover in the group that wanted the members to take over. He argued that the short-term burden of raising the purchase price was likely to be far outweighed by increased subscriptions under a new owner.

In 1976, annual membership had been set at £45 a year for men and £40 for women.

An extraordinary general meeting was held to discuss the sale of the club and there was unanimous support for buying it. There was a proposal that members could make loans in multiples of £50 towards the cost, compensated by a proportionate reduction in the annual subscription. Dennis Millward, who had taken over as club president from Glen Ogilvie, tendered an offer £80,000 on behalf of the members. It was rejected, but the asking price reduced to £122,500.

Should the members have seized the opportunity? Bob Curle believed that if everyone put in £500 they could have done it. But that is well over £3,000 in today's money, and many could simply not afford it, or were too old to want to make such an investment in a future they would not share.

Hugh Curle, Bob's son, said that at one point his father was one of four members prepared to invest £30,000 each, but one pulled out.

In any event, the deal fell through. The committee concluded that the asking price was beyond reach, a position overwhelmingly supported by a proxy vote. There remained the issue of the silver trophies, valued at £3,000 by the liquidator. He was told they could not be sold as part of the club's assets without reference to the original donors or their successors.

If the failure to gain control of the club remains a matter for debate among the more senior members, so too does the role of the man who eventually bought it.

The late Colin White, who created carvings in the clubhouse and the starter's hut. His bench on the 1st tee carries the inscription: 'Keep it on the short stuff'.

FIELD OF DREAMS

Alec Stenson, who bought the golf club from the Ogilvie family in 1982. Alec died in 1999, shortly after selling to the current owners.

His name was Alec Stenson, an astute and hard-nosed businessman who made his fortune when he co-founded the Kwik Fit tyre and repair company with the Scottish entrepreneur Sir Tom Farmer. He already owned Aldenham Golf and Country Club near Watford.

The Stensons had moved to Florida in 1979 after doctors recommended a warmer climate for their son David, who suffered from asthma. Alec commuted between America and Britain on Concord, and the family kept the holiday home they owned in Thorpeness. They enjoyed golf, and Alec's wife, Anne, had been the Kent junior champion.

Alec Stenson believed the golf club at Thorpeness could be turned into an attractive resort, where guests would be given priority. Many members viewed the plan with consternation. In November 1982, the ladies' committee reported that resignations had greatly reduced numbers. The main club committee also noted that several members were withholding payment 'on principle' as the deadline for subscription renewal approached. Membership records of the time no longer exist, but there is no doubt that there was a significant exodus from the club.

What is clear is that changes were quickly introduced. The annual subscription, as Bob Curle had warned, was increased to £150 for men and £120 for women. The artisan section, viewed as an anachronism by the new owner, was disbanded and its members invited to join the main club without paying an entrance fee. Dress regulations were relaxed too. The old jacket-and-tie rule was replaced by 'smart casual'.

The clubhouse was expanded and altered. An annexe with 22 bedrooms was built, more rooms were added to the old Dormy House and the Ogilvie Restaurant opened. Starting times were introduced on the course, with priority during the main part of the day given to hotel guests. The restrictions on fourballs were lifted and the course became busier, and slower. There was grumbling and discontent, and some

🍺 Cheers! Ray Foreman, three times club champion, had a clean sweep of the major Thorpeness trophies, finishing with the Silver Frigate, in 2015. One of the club's great characters, Ray died in 2020.

acrimonious confrontations with the new owner. However, when Neville Griffin took over as manager he became a popular figure.

The spirit of the club survived throughout it all. The silver trophies retained pride above leather armchairs and sofas in an oak-lined bar where large gins flowed freely, as they always had.

The course record of 67, established back in the mid-60s, was finally equalled in the 1982 Ogilvie Shield. The card was returned by Stuart Goodman, who started with a birdie and slipped up with a bogey on only one hole. The following year Stuart left for Ipswich Golf Club and went on to play a leading role in county golf in both Suffolk and Norfolk.

Three years later, Jon Marks of Woodbridge Golf Club enjoyed the first of his three victories in the Silver Frigate. The 1985 event was restricted to one round because of torrential rain and Jon scored a 67 before the heavens opened. It was one of four Suffolk course records that he held at various times.

The Frigate has had some notable winners, perhaps none more so that the late Derek Hammond-Giles. His two victories were separated by an astonishing 36 years. Derek first won the trophy in 1952, then again in 1988. His handicap of 18 had not changed.

The club championship was introduced in 1985. It was soon dominated by Martin Youngs, the son of Trevor. He had joined Thorpeness as a junior in 1976 but became the assistant professional at Aldeburgh Golf Club. After regaining his amateur status, Martin went back to Thorpeness. He was club champion five times between 1988 and 1994.

Ray Foreman could not equal that record, but he is remembered as one of the great stalwarts of the club, and one if its best players. He was club champion in 1992, 1997 and 2002, and during a membership that spanned several decades won each one the 'major' Thorpeness trophies. He completed the set with the Silver Frigate in 2015. Ray liked to joke that to match the grander club members he had added letters after his own name: PD, for painter and decorator. He ran a business in Snape, where he grew up. Ray died in 2020.

Club champions are awarded a silver salver mounted on a carved wooden backing. It was designed by Colin White, whose carvings surround the clock on the starter's hut. Colin trained as an apprentice boat builder in the Isle of Wight, joined the Navy and eventually settled in Suffolk. He was a popular member of the club and after his death in 1994 his widow presented his carving of an eagle as the Colin White Trophy. It is contested each year by the Seniors' section before their Christmas lunch.

Alec Stenson himself played on the course when he was visiting, and being the owner had its advantages. Members liked to say that any area of rough that swallowed up his ball would soon be cut back.

The proprietor certainly wanted the course to be more friendly, not least to keep play moving. The modifications he made are now common practice across East Anglia, with gorse thinned and trees removed to allow more light to reach greens and fairways.

Despite the changes, Thorpeness remained a formidable challenge. A booklet produced at the time described it as 'not only most enjoyable for the average player, but a real test for the scratch man'.

The Stenson reign, unlike that of the Ogilvies, was short-lived. In 1991 the golf club was put up for sale. Buyers were advised the land was valued at £7,000 per acre and that the number of guest bedrooms could be increased to 60. Offers were invited in the region of £5m.

The members once again debated the possibility of buying at least a stake in the club. A special committee was formed, financial options investigated, and discussions held. But if raising £122,500 10 years earlier might have been achievable, the figures now were simply too high.

At a meeting with Alec Stenson on December 30, 1991, the committee was advised that the club was valued at £4m. Further talks were pointless. The committee tried to strike an optimistic note by declaring: "The possible change of ownership need not necessarily be a cause of concern to members."

It was to be five more years before that change took place.

Alec Stenson remains a controversial figure at Thorpeness Golf Club, but without him it might very well have faced extinction. He died in 1999. His last venture was a hotel in the Bahamas, run by his son David until it was destroyed by a hurricane. His sister, Sheila Pickering, was given life membership when he sold the club. She lived in Thorpeness and remained an active member of the ladies' section until her death in 2019. Anne Stenson, Alec's widow, died in 2020. Hers was one of the many lives claimed by the Coronavirus pandemic.

In Thorpeness, the Stensons left behind a golf club that had faced more than its fair share of uncertainty. The next stage of its 100-year journey was about to begin.

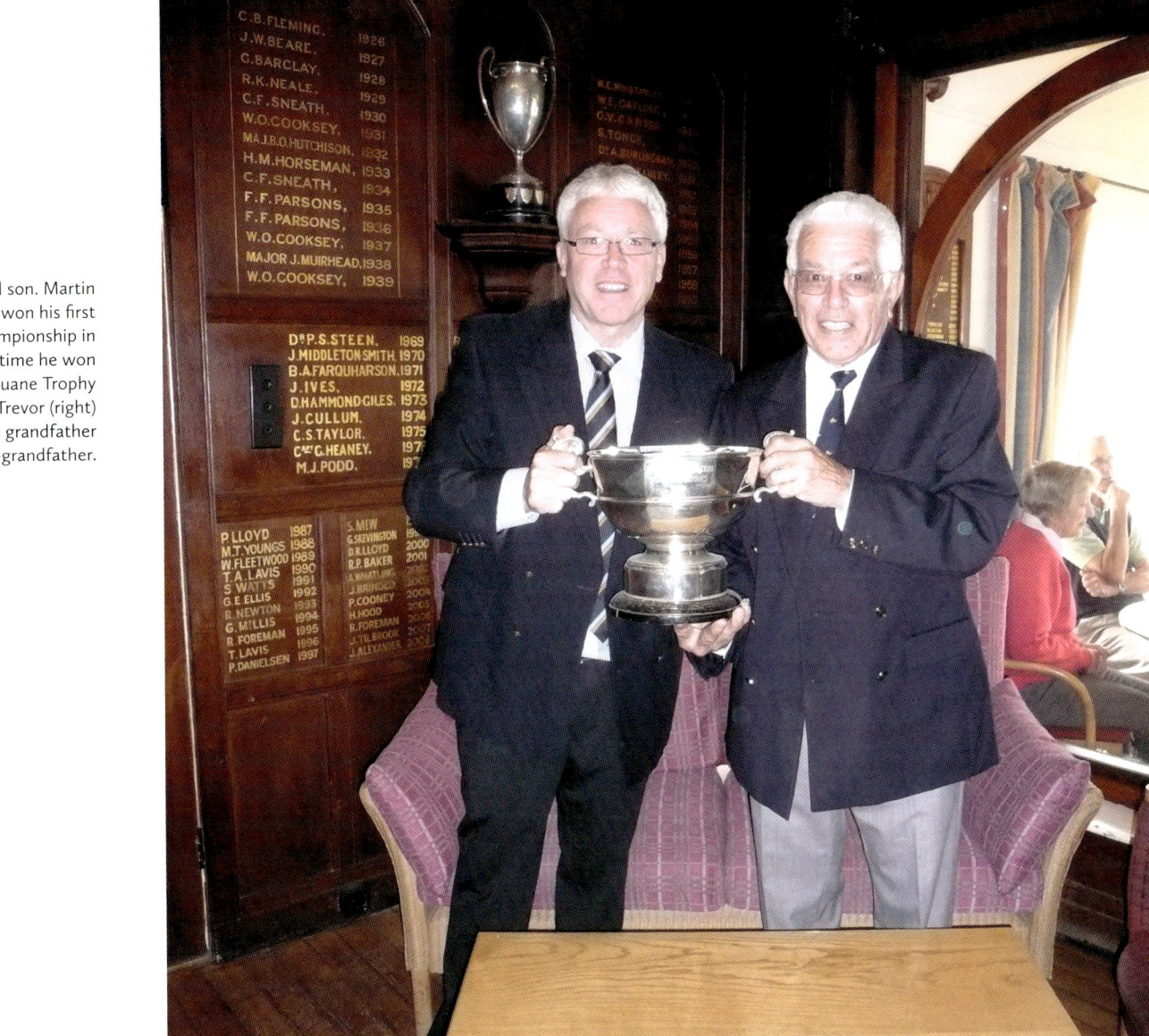

Thorpeness Golf Club: The First 100 Years **1922-2022**

Father and son. Martin Youngs (left) won his first club championship in 1988. By the time he won the 2013 Ruane Trophy with dad Trevor (right) they were a grandfather and great-grandfather.

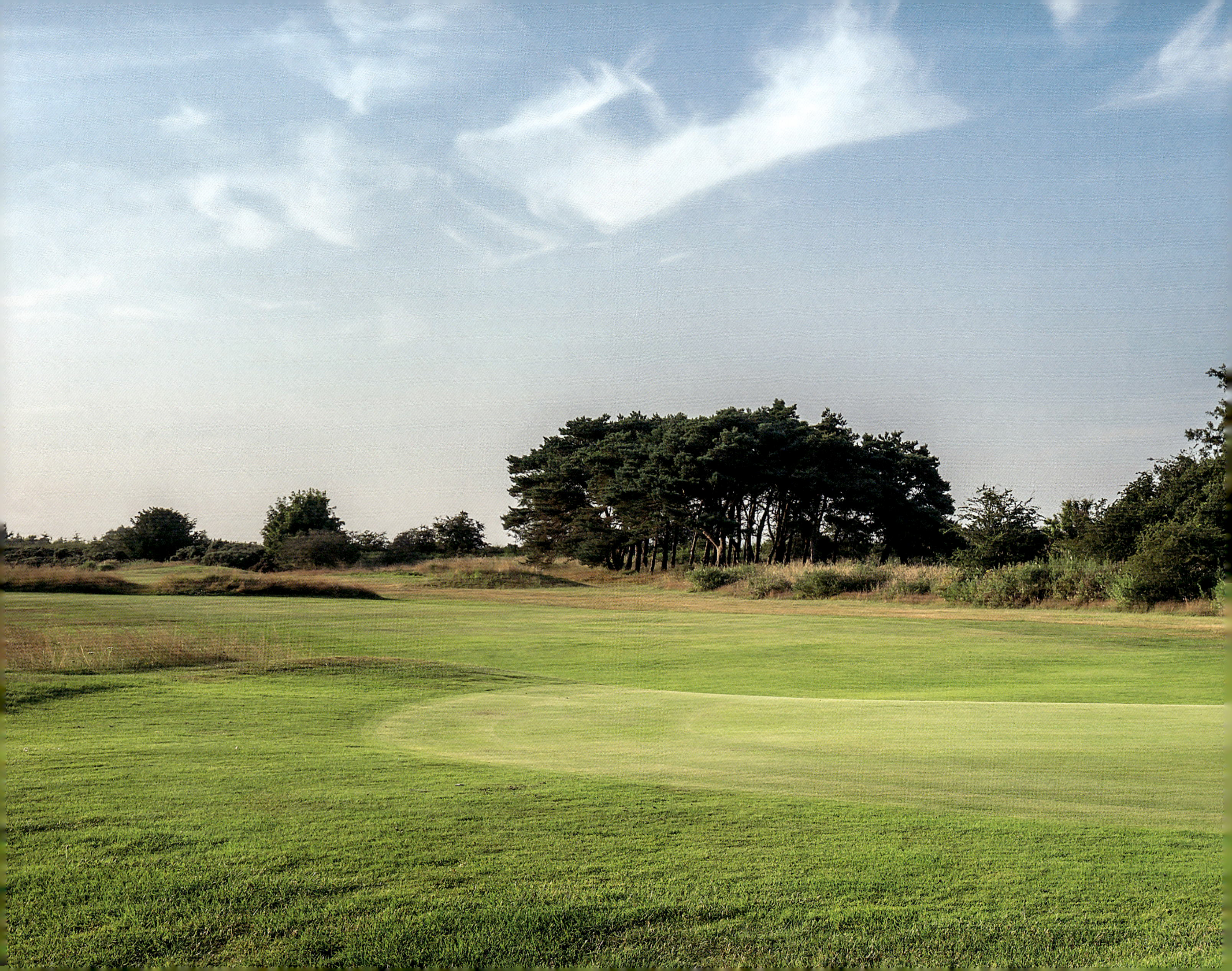

Thorpeness in the summer months: the 11th green and fairway under typically expansive Suffolk skies.

FIELD OF DREAMS

Chapter 5

THE NEW MILLENNIUM
APPROACHING A CENTURY

Frank Hill was the pro at Thorpeness for 20 years until he retired in 2012. This picture was taken in the 1960s. Looking on is former Ryder Cup captain Harry Weetman.

It started with a chance meeting between two men in Aldeburgh. Guy Heald was a foreign exchange specialist in the world of international banking, with a career that had taken him from London to New York and Tokyo. Tim Rowan-Robinson had spent his working life in the hospitality industry, rising to become managing director of the Whitbread hotel division.

Both were golfers and they shared a love of Suffolk going back to childhood. Guy had spent his summer holidays in Aldeburgh and was introduced to the game by his father. Tim started to collect golfing trophies as a schoolboy. His name appears in the Thorpeness club records in 1960 when, at the age of 10, he won the under-12 section of the county junior championships. Glen Ogilvie was among those he beat. Tim won the same event the following year, and in 1974 was the Suffolk amateur matchplay champion. At that meeting in Aldeburgh many years

Glory days: Current director of golf Christine Langford was a pioneer of the Ladies European Tour, and topped the Order of Merit in 1979.

later, the prospect of owning the golf club was irresistible. Thorpeness and Aldeburgh Hotels was formed, and the club became the first in a portfolio of six Suffolk properties. The company was later re-branded as The Hotel Folk.

Accommodation at Thorpeness was extended by adding eight rooms to Braid Lodge behind the pro shop, and six above the Ogilvie Restaurant. Tim Rowan-Robinson wanted to attract better golfers. He believed that cut-price packages in the past had brought in visitors for whom the challenge of Thorpeness was simply too much. Rounds had become unacceptably slow and the course had deteriorated. It had affected morale among members and numbers were shrinking.

The balance between guests and members at Thorpeness has always been tricky. The new owners extended reserved tee times for members by 30 minutes in the morning and, as the nation prepared to celebrate the Queen's 50 years on the throne, a Jubilee membership scheme was introduced as an alternative to the annual subscription. It allowed golfers to buy a book of vouchers to be used each time a game was played.

Club treasurer Ian Laird had been in many discussions with Alec Stenson and knew better than most how hard a negotiator he could be. There was, he said, an instantaneous improvement in relations with the proprietors when the club changed hands.

FIELD OF DREAMS

There was the new club professional for this latest era. Frank Hill was to spend 20 years at Thorpeness and saw out his golfing career there. Frank was a schoolboy when he picked up a right-handed golf club with a with his left-handed cricket grip and fell in love with the game. He got a job cleaning shoes at a club in Nottinghamshire and was immediately classified as an assistant pro. He had been training for a career in catering but gave it up for golf. His mum, he said, 'went ballistic'.

Over the years that followed, Frank was the professional at six golf clubs. He played in four Open Championships and on the European Seniors Tour. In 2006 he won the PGA Super Seniors.

His best score at Thorpeness, a 64, came during a friendly captain and pro challenge match and did not count as a course record. Many Thorpeness members honed their golfing skills under Frank's tutelage. He laid great store in a good grip and a sensible approach. Thorpeness, he advised, is not a course on which to attempt rash shots.

The course was to become even more challenging. After James Braid and Ken Cotton came designer Ken Moodie, working with Frank and course manager Ian Willet to add new bunkers, a fresh look and extra yardage. The biggest change was to the 9th, a 439-yard par 4. It was re-modelled as a par 5, measuring 489 yards from the white tees, and 534 from the blue. Thorpeness was now a course of nearly 6,500 yards from those blue tees.

The work was completed in 2012, and to mark the occasion Thorpeness was chosen with neighbouring Aldeburgh to co-host the English Seniors Amateur Stroke Play Championship. The opening round was at Thorpeness, where many of the country's top senior golfers struggled in the bracken and gorse. Seventeen of them failed to break 90, and two returned cards of 96. The eventual winner, Alan Squires of Oldham, followed a 75 at Thorpeness with rounds of 77 and 69 at Aldeburgh.

There was more recognition for Thorpeness that year. It was chosen as the

Head greenkeeper William 'Wallace' Wilson, far left, and his team. Hotel Folk have invested heavily in machinery, and plan significant improvements to the course.

greenest course in Britain with the gold medal in the Golf Environment Awards. In Michael Wood's 2010 history, the club's ecological adviser, Ray Hardinge, had written about the 'hauntingly beautiful landscape' and the variety of wildlife to which it was home. He was emphatic about the need to preserve that environment, and his words have been heeded. The course is a haven for birds and there are designated hibernation areas for adders, frogs and toads.

It was Frank Hill's assistant, Chris Oldrey, who coached the club's growing number of junior members, lining them up on the practice ground on a Saturday morning for training sessions. But if Chris was the teacher, the indomitable Pauline Hislop was the inspiration.

Pauline had joined in 1980 and as the new millennium dawned she began to feel the club was in need of new blood. Her solution was a campaign that took her to schools throughout the area to champion the sport of golf. Saturday lessons were offered at one pound a head, and juniors could become members for £25 a year. Pauline took charge of the etiquette side of the game, teaching young players how to conduct themselves during a round of golf. When she took them from the practice ground to the course she travelled in a buggy, many of her golfing proteges running behind her. The juniors Pauline Hislop inspired have made their mark at Thorpeness.

Jack Cuthbert was just seven when he first picked up a golf club. By the time he played in a junior stableford in September, 2015, he was 15. Jack hit his drive on the 17th over the hill and into what he thought must be a bunker. It was in the hole. The 17th is a 277-yard par 4, giving Jack five stableford points. That extraordinary hole in one was part of a round of 70, a record on the new layout.

Harry Brinded had clocked up 49 stableford points as a nine-year-old in 2015. His handicap then was 37. Five years later, at the age of 14, he was down to five and became the youngest club champion when rounds of 77 and 75 beat his father into second place.

🏠 Pauline Hislop and her original Thorpeness Juniors. L-R, back row: Sam Newson, Sam May, Josh Spall, Will Stebbings, George Batho, Jack Levermore. Middle row: Fionn O'Reilly, Ben Morris, Molly Newson, Pauline Hislop, Jack Cuthbert, James Cook, Guy Maynard. Front: Mary Cuthbert, Joseph Dix.

FIELD OF DREAMS

Dame Laura Davies drove the green on the 322-yard 1st in the 2019 Ladies European Tour pro-am. But she was soon in the deep rough. "If you're wayward on this course, good luck," she said.

Harry's score of 70 in a medal in June 2021 matched Jack Cuthbert's course record.

Dominic Rudd had just turned 13 when he won the Silver Frigate in 2018, the youngest player ever to do so. His round of 74 gave him a nett score of 68.

In the ladies' section, Molly Newson and Mary Cuthbert, Jack's sister, appear regularly in the lists of competition winners. In August 2020, Molly shot a 79 against a par of 74, the lowest score recorded by a lady member at Thorpeness.

The round was finished with a flourish: an eagle three on the 18th, a par 5 on the ladies' card.

But no mention of junior achievements at Thorpeness would be complete without the story of Juliette Coffey, a 13-year-old from Woodbridge. Juliette was playing off 37 when she won the stableford section of the 2018 Bell Cup. She had a disastrous 'no return' on the one hole on which she received three strokes. On the remaining 17, however, she got six pars and a birdie on the way to accumulating 53 points. The record books appear to contain no better stableford score in the club's first 100 years.

At the other end of the age spectrum, a new seniors' section was created and quickly flourished. It was born out of the Wednesday Club, which, under the guidance the late Bob Trevelyan, had developed into a popular roll-up. Players would meet in the locker room and draw cards for playing partners. There was a suggestion, eventually rejected, that the group should be re-named the Trogs – the Thorpeness Retired Old Golfers Society.

The Seniors are early risers. They have roll-ups three days a week with a 7.45am call. They compete against other clubs and have regular competitions of their own. The Trevelyan Cup is contested over six rounds, with the best three to count. By the time of the centenary, there were more than 80 names on the seniors' membership list.

Every golfer knows their game will eventually deteriorate, but one of the finest players Thorpeness has seen was in

On the Swilcan Bridge. Joyce Booth and Lucie Reeve finished third in the final of the Coronation Foursomes at St Andrews in September, 2021. They were the first Thorpeness ladies to reach the finals of an event that attracts hundreds of golfers from around the country.

his prime when he suffered a cruel setback. Like Martin Youngs a decade earlier, Jamie Philpot had been an assistant professional at Aldeburgh, regained his amateur status and joined Thorpeness. His handicap was plus one and Jamie won the club championship five years in a row starting in 2004. He added a sixth victory in 2010.

His winning streak was brought to a halt by a medical condition which forces the fingers to become bent into a flexed position. It is frequently hereditary and although surgery can help, there is no cure. Jamie eventually started playing again, swinging the club with a baseball grip, and was able to get his score back down to the seventies.

Frank Hill retired in 2015 and was replaced by someone who had also started the game with stars in their eyes when Christine Langford was appointed as Director of Golf.

Christine had decided to turn professional after winning the 1974 English Girls' Championships at the age of 16. Like Frank, she faced fierce maternal

FIELD OF DREAMS

Proud father, victorious son. Harry Brinded became the youngest club champion when he won the title in 2020 at the age of 14. Dad Harry was beaten into second place.

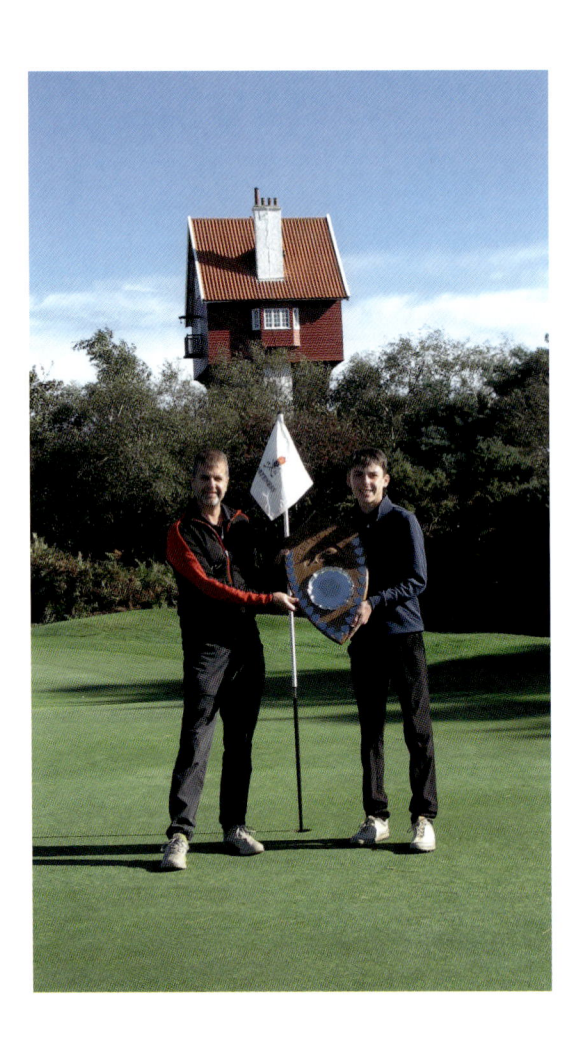

opposition. Nice girls, she was told, do not do it for money.

Christine's dream took her first to the LPGA Tour in the United States and then to the Ladies' European Tour, where she won four tournaments and topped the 1979 Order of Merit. She was a founder member, and later chair, of the Women's Professional Golfers Association.

In 1988, Christine made British golfing history when she was appointed professional at Clevedon Golf Club in Somerset. She became the first female professional at a private members' club. Of those 1,000 members, only 100 were women. They were not allowed on the course before 11.30 in the morning.

Christine established herself as a leading golf teacher over the years. She coached the 2000 Welsh national ladies' team, two of whom represented Great Britain in the Curtis Cup. She has worked in the United States and Spain and run annual golf tours to Bermuda. She teaches the old-fashioned way, without computers or video, and her philosophy is simple: when the lesson is over golfers should enjoy the game more.

The history of Thorpeness Golf Club is punctuated with moments of crisis, and as its centenary approached there was yet another. Coronavirus disrupted golf across the country, but for the hospitality industry it was a particularly harsh blow. Lockdowns forced the Thorpeness guest rooms to be closed for a total of 282 days.

As the second lockdown was lifted in 2021, the club prepared to welcome the return of summer golf with a prestigious tournament: The Logan Trophy is the English mid-amateur championship for golfers over the age of 35.

The eventual winner, Philip Ridden of City of Newcastle, shared the first-round lead with Andy Grimwood of St Neots. Their scores of 68 were records on the par-70 course, but it was a tough day for many of those left in their wake.

Cards were littered with eights and nines, several competitors returned scores in the nineties and one was forced to walk

Thorpeness Golf Club: The First 100 Years **1922-2022**

🏠 The Thorpeness Seniors, class of 2021. More than 80 club members are registered to play in the Seniors. It's not for late risers. The roll-up starts at 7.45 in the morning.

in after six holes having run out of golf balls. Thorpeness member Richard Weaver completed the first hole only to discover he had fifteen clubs in his bag. The two-stroke penalty for the extra club turned a five into seven, but Richard still finished with a 74.

As the cloud of the pandemic lifted, owner Guy Heald began to consider the future. Thorpeness, he believed, should be given a new lease of life, and restored to former glories.

He envisages the resort as an eco-friendly destination to tempt more families to spend their summers on the Suffolk coast. At its heart, the golf club will be given better accommodation and facilities, for both members and guests. The course will be improved accordingly, fairways and greens manicured to pristine condition. And there will be a nine-hole course to add to the appeal. It is a blueprint for an exciting future.

One hundred years after Glencairn Stuart Ogilvie turned his vision to reality, Thorpeness is still a field of dreams. 🏠

The par-4 13th features a green that sits temptingly towards the approaching golfer.

» The short 2nd returns towards the clubhouse and is a handsome, downhill par 3.